Miss Molly & Me

Best Friends Forever

ISBN: 978-1-60800-011-1
Library of Congress Control Number: 2011910342

Design and layout by Pamela Haines
American Literary Publishing
Lancaster, PA
717 239 0490
www.americanliterarypublishing.com

Printed by Yurchak Printing Inc.
Lancaster, PA
www.yurchak.com

Designed, published and printed in the
United States of America

Miss Molly & Me

Best Friends Forever

By Stacie Randall Self

American Literary Publishing
Lancaster, PA

Contents

Loving Molly

It was a hot, sticky day on August 31,1994. We were living in the beautiful waterfront neighborhood of Royal Harbour Estates, located in Ooltewah, Tennessee. It was one of those days the heat made your feet stick to the earth; it was difficult to walk and breathe at the same time.

That day was Carolyn Alexander's neighborhood brunch. All of the ladies who stayed home were invited to come for a visit to enjoy her homemade chicken salad and all of the Southern "fixin's," including sweet ice tea. We all loved to go to Carolyn's home. She was a wonderful cook, and her home was always beautifully decorated. She was a joy to be around.

I remember looking at my watch and thinking it was almost 1:30 p.m. and about time to leave. Annie, my Golden Retriever, was due for a check-up at the local veterinary office. Annie was one of those Golden Retrievers who loved the water and was always wet and a bit smelly from the lake water.

I packed up my belongings, thanked Carolyn for a lovely morning, and drove to the top of the street to our home to pick up Miss Annie. Annie was waiting patiently for me to come spend some time with her. She jumped into the car and off we went, down the long winding drive that led us up a hill and out of the neighborhood.

At the bottom of the hill across from the neighborhood swimming pool was a little white, fluffy dog running in the street, right in front of my car. Wow… that was close. I slammed on the brakes.

The poor little dog looked so hot and tired and worn out. Another man stopped his car across from me and asked if I knew anything about the dog.

"No," I answered.

The man had heard this little dog was seen running from neighborhood to neighborhood.

"I think I have a lost puppy," I called back to him. "I am on my way to the vet's office now with

Annie, so I will take one more with me."

Slowly getting out of the car, I reached down and picked up this little ball of fur and held her tightly, close to my shoulder. She seemed to relax. I put her on the front seat of the car and drove a few miles into town to the White Oak Animal Clinic. I wondered how she would do in the car… well, within a few minutes she curled up in the middle of my large pocketbook and took a nap, letting the cool air from the air conditioning blow across her face. She is so cute I thought, and she must belong to someone in the town of Ooltewah.

The vet's office was busy, but everyone stopped what they were doing to take a look at this little dog. She was matted and hungry.

"The best thing would be to leave her here overnight and let Dr. Dave Miller take a look at her and run a couple of tests to see if she is

Carolyn and Bob Alexander

healthy," Michelle, the vet tech, said. "She is dehydrated and probably has been wandering around for several days. We will run some tests and send her home with you in a day or two."

The next two days went by rather fast. By Friday afternoon Mark, my husband, would be home from his trip. I waited to see if he wanted to go down to the clinic and visit with this little ball of fur that resembled the end of a mop.

Mark ran late Friday evening, so Saturday morning had to work with his schedule.

"The clinic closes at noon," I yelled to him. Just take a look and see what you think …," my voice trailed off. About one hour later, home came Mark with Molly in his arms.

We soon nicknamed her the "Molly Mop," from one of the nursery rhymes my husband remembered from his childhood. She had very long hair that was matted and was the color most groomers would call apricot. She really looked like a little mop.

Miss Molly the Mop

Adoption Time

The next couple of weeks were trying for us. The little Molly girl did not like sleeping in the cardboard box Mark made for her in the garage. She cried all night long and chewed on everything in her path. She cried for weeks.

One morning we went out to check on her and noticed she had chewed her way out of the box and eaten part of the steps leading into the kitchen. She also ate part of the wall around the door. We then noticed daylight was creeping its way into the dark garage, which meant the bottom flashing of the garage door had been ingested. Wow! That little girl had strong teeth.

Maybe this was not a good idea. Maybe she really did belong to someone else, and we needed to advertise on the radio and in the newspaper that we had found a lost little dog.

I found Luther, the radio announcer on the local radio station that advertised lost pets all day. I gave him the location she was found and a description of her looks. She really was a Cockapoo. He broadcast all day and night. He kept calling me back for the next couple of days to say no one called to claim this little ball of fur.

My mom and dad came to visit the week we found Molly. Mom and I drove around the lake and surrounding neighborhoods and knocked on doors. This little dog was so cute; she must belong to someone or live on someone's farm.

One of my dear friends, Ameta Stephens, was our local pharmacist. She had an adorable little Shitzu named Chelsea. Ameta knew an elderly woman who was looking for a little dog to keep her company.

The woman offered to put up a fence in her backyard and come pick her up in a week or two.

That seemed like a great idea. I also tried my potty training classes with Molly, but in the mean time I realized she was confused with the outside world and the inside world.

This would be a challenge for the elderly woman. Molly was not house trained and only about six months old. She chewed on everything in the house and the garage. She chased cars, too. But this little dog was so cute and was developing a wonderful personality.

No one answered the lost dog ads, and the big day was here for our little Molly to go visit her new home and live with the elderly lady. Guess who started to cry? I could not let her go away. Something had bonded between the two of us, and I believe Mark felt it, too.

I thought Annie, our Golden Retriever, was frustrated with having a stray dog in the house, but she was such a kind-natured dog. She would eventually accept her.

My wonderful friend Ameta & Chelsea

Amber and Stacie

Annie had been bought from Carol and Frank Lorch in Clifton Park, New York. They were the best Golden Retriever breeders in that area. We enjoyed their company, and their Golden Retrievers were the best! The Lorch's were the best friends to call on if you had any medical questions about dogs.

Our new addition, Miss Molly, was not house broken, peed everywhere, and just loved to sleep at the foot of our bed. So much for the cardboard box in the garage.

Amber and Stacie at the boathouse

Amber at the lake house

New Beginning in Birchwood, Tennessee

One of our moves was to Birchwood, Tennessee. Our house was in the Birchwood area and about nineteen miles from town. It was so far from town we had to take a cooler with us to go to the grocery store. There were only six homes in this neighborhood. The driveway was hidden from the main road. It was a beautiful setting on the lake.

At this time, we also owned a cat named Pepper. Pepper was a stray kitten. She was very independent and loving and spent most of her time lounging on the back deck that overlooked the lake. It was really a great place for pets to run and enjoy the outdoors.

Pepper's mother was a stray cat that lived in an old fishing boat. We had named her Tiger. The mother cat had made a bed for her kittens from an old sleeping bag that was wrapped around the hot water heater in the garage. She had torn the sleeping bag down and put it on the floor for the kittens to have a warm, comfortable bed. It was wintertime, and four little kittens had to be fed and kept warm until we could find homes for them.

One of the neighbors had a family member who owned a veterinary clinic in town, so the little ones had good homes immediately. Pepper, the friendliest kitten, stayed with us.

Mark and baby Pepper

Pepper seemed to tolerate Molly. She would lie on her back and let the dogs sniff her belly. She loved tummy rubs and snuggling with us on the bed in the evenings.

Molly seemed to enjoy the cat, too. I thought our little family was growing with four-legged kids.

The more time I spent with Molly, I realized she would be hard to house train. She may have spent the first six months of her little life on one of the farms, but I was determined the rest of her life she would be loved and cared for in the comfort of our home.

Miss Pepper and her mom, Tiger

Diesel Engines

Molly settled into her routine of sleeping part of the time in her crate when we had to go to work and could not watch her around the clock. As soon as one of us was home, she was in the house and happy to be part of the family.

As she learned her way around our rather large yard, we discovered her love of trucks. It was not just any truck driving around the neighborhood…it had to be a large truck that made the distinct diesel sound that stops you in your tracks.

Our home sat below the street level, because most of the lots where sloped to back down to the river. The driveway was long, steep, and curved. The steep part was right in front of the house; a bit difficult to walk up, let alone run after a dog.

Molly had no trouble chasing a truck up the driveway and into the street. She ran right along side of the UPS or FED EX trucks and looked back to see if we followed her. It was terrifying to watch and impossible to stop her. Our screams were heard up and down street, "Molly stop, stop..," but she kept on running.

It was time to leash train her and walk her on a pathway down by the water. Mark had a new project: to clear the walking path in the woods next to our house. The path was old and worn out. The only people who used it were fishermen or kids who took short cuts from home or hiked down to the local fishing hole.

After several hours of clearing and weed-whacking the pathway it was time to walk with Annie and Molly on a new adventure. The dogs loved the trail, and even the cat, Pepper, would join us in the evenings.

Family Outing on the Lake

The Skunk

One evening in late summer we decided to walk the main road through the Royal Harbour subdivision. My parents, Joan and Dan, were visiting, and we all took off for a walk down to the neighborhood swimming pool.

The dog leashes were wrapped around our shoulders and necks, not on the dogs. The dogs were by our sides and walked freely.

The neighborhood pool was at the far end of the road was a good hike for us. About half way down the street and around a sharp left turn there was a great view of the bottom of the road before it turned off to the right and out of sight.

I guess Molly and Annie saw it before the rest of us. Sitting in the middle of the street was a black and white animal. A cat? No, a skunk just sat there in the middle of the road and waited for all of us to walk into its lovely scent. It was more then a scent… it was like an oily, burning spray that covered the side of my neck and ran down my clothes. The dogs were covered in this mess, and so was I. Ugh!

Thank goodness I had remembered to bring the key to the pool with me. The pool had a phone inside the gate and a water hose that came in handy to hose down two dogs and me, the owner. I called Mark from the pool.

"Please, please, bring me a change of clothes and tomato juice for the dogs. I have been sprayed by a skunk, and so were Annie and Molly. "I think I am going to pass out," I said.

Mark jumped into his car and rescued all of us with new clothes and lots of tomato juice. I jumped into the pool to cool off, and Mark unraveled the hoses by the clubhouse and sprayed down the dogs.

My parents were able to walk us all home, where the dog cleaning continued in our driveway.

The smell lasted for days. I called Dr. Dave Miller again for suggestions as to what would work well to kill the smell.

"Come into my office, after hours, so you don't clear out the waiting room, and I will have something mixed in the lab that will help you," he said.

Whatever the aqua blue liquid was in that little vial, it worked. We all bathed in it, (not together!) and it finally cleared the air in our home. What a week...all of the collars were thrown away, and new leashes were bought for all.

Dad and Annie

My parents enjoyed spending time with us at the lake house. The backyard was like a summer camp. There was a boat for skiing that belonged to my dad but was shared by us all. There were also a canoe, a large jet ski, and a fishing boat.

Annie, the Golden Retriever, loved the water and the boats. She learned to jet ski by watching us ride, one driver in front of the other. One afternoon the jet ski sat next to the dock with the engine idling slowly. The next minute Annie was sitting on the front seat. Her left front paw was on the steering column, and her right paw hit the green "go" button. Wow… there goes my dog… she was out of the harbor and steering for the main channel.

We swam behind her but could not catch up. "Go get her," I yelled to Mark.

"Let's get the ski boat and go after her," Mark yelled back to me.

We jumped into the boat and headed out to stop her before another boat got in her way. We pulled up next to her, and Mark hopped on the jet ski with her and stopped the whole situation from getting worse. What a dog! She was so happy to see us. She was also proud of her moment of independence on the water.

"We are definitely going to keep a watchful eye on her and keep her locked up in the house the next time we go boating," Mark added.

Well, the next time was not that far away. We decided to take the boat out again with my parents a couple of days later. Molly was in the house, and the house was locked. Annie was tied on a leash by the boat garage in the back yard.

Our family headed out for an afternoon of boating. We were gone a half-hour and headed for the main channel. All of a sudden there in the water, about a quarter of a mile out in the neighborhood slew, was Annie. She swam frantically trying to catch up to the boat and us.

"Oh man, that's my dog," I yelled.

We turned the Ski Ray around and headed toward Annie. She was a great swimmer. Mark put the ladder down on the back of the boat. She climbed up the steps all by herself and jumped into the boat, and in a split second she shook the lake water all over the four of us!

"What a smart girl, I said.

She had to stay in the house with Molly on our next outing, so she could not follow us out into the river. It just was not safe. I had never seen such a strong will in a dog to go swimming and boating. But I was learning. Boy, was I learning!

Mark and his friend, Ron working on the boat with Dad overseeing the project

Mark, Dad and Stacie and Mom starting up the boat!

Annie the new baby!

Trapped!

We were transferred from the Schenectady, New York area to Chattanooga, Tennessee the year of 1992. This was our second adventure to Tennessee. Mark grew up in Athens, Tennessee a small town located between Chattanooga and Knoxville. Our Golden Retriever, Annie was about three years old when we moved to our second lake house in Tennessee.

Annie was high energy and loved water. The lake house was perfect for her. She learned fast all about boating, canoeing, jet skiing, and staying muddy and dirty most of the day. She was always into everything and doing it face first. But she was a love and a joy to be around. I replaced more bedspreads, towels and blankets than I could ever count.

During one of the Christmas holidays we decided to head to Lancaster, Pennsylvania for a visit with my family. It took several days to load up the car with luggage, gifts, doggie beds, and food for the trip.

The trip was approximately 12 hours from Chattanooga, Tennessee to Lancaster, Pennsylvania. Annie and Molly always enjoyed the overnight stays at hotels along the way. They usually ate well, sausage and egg biscuits were a favorite. Of course, real dog food was mixed in throughout the day to keep a healthy diet.

The roadside rests were the best way to stretch your legs and walk the pups around a parking lot. We tried to get to my home in two days…that was about my time limit with the dogs in the car. We made decent time and arrived to a cold and snowy winter wonderland.

Mark decided to walk Annie and Molly back into the farmland behind my parents' home. It was a beautiful old farm with the long, winding driveway that seemed to go on forever. The walk was on Christmas Eve Day. It was an early morning walk for the three of them. I was resting in the guest room after the long drive up north. The next moment I heard Mark's voice yelling for help.

"What in the world is going on," I said, as I jumped out of the bed.

Mark yelled for me to call the emergency veterinary clinic. Molly had gotten her leg caught in a fox trap.

Mark pulled the entire trap out of the ground, stake and all, including the raw meat that was packed into the middle of it as bait. Mark thought the meat was actually Molly's flesh. We had never seen such a scary sight. We could not tell what part of her leg was injured or what part was just the raw, ground meat.

We wrapped her in a blanket and ran to the nearest clinic for help. The emergency vet unsnapped the trap with help from Mark. Molly was the luckiest dog in the world. The meat had actually protected her little paw and shielded it from injury. She was sore, but there was not one deep cut on her leg or paw.

Molly had a special guardian angel with her that morning. She was blessed and certainly given extra treats the rest of the visit. She had a little limp but overall was fine. This was a good Christmas! Annie was happy her little friend was going to be well.

Mark went back to the farm to speak with the farmer about the use of traps in a mostly residential area. They were illegal in an area so close to homes. The farmer promised us the traps would all be removed in the next day or two.

I would have hated to see someone else go through that experience, either with a pet or a child. The neighborhood school was on the edge of the farmer's field. That was not a safe place for traps of any kind.

Mom and Uncle Neal with Annie and me waiting for pot roast

The remainder of the vacation we visited with family and friends and, of course, enjoyed Mom's world famous pot roast, the best in the county. The dogs enjoyed a little dish of the pot roast with their dog food. Yes, the holidays were fun…especially when mom cooked up goodies in the kitchen for man and dogs!

I must say my mom was the dog lover in the family. She grew up in Malverne, New York with a little white Cocker Spaniel. His name was Laddie. He was my mom's best friend.

My mom lived with her grandmother, Nana Montgomery, who was a seamstress. Mom always enjoyed spending time walking her dog along the tree-lined streets of Malverne.

Mom's parents were separated and lived apart from my mom during her younger days. My mom spent her childhood years being ill with ulcers.

She had her best friend, Marilyn Crabe to grow up with and spend the high school years together. I remember Mom told me that one-day her dog just disappeared. It was garbage day, and the dog had gotten out and was gone in the blink of an eye. I know how scary and upsetting that must have been for a little girl.

She often told us stories about her dog eating sewing pins. I had never heard of a dog eating straight pins. That must have been the unhealthy side of the sewing business, having a dog at your feet.

I have twin sisters, and both of them have cats. Nancy was more of a dog person, but her cat, Nic, was awesome. He really acted like a dog. He would greet you at the door and rub all over you during your visit. If you did not let Nic "love on you," he would go in the other room, lie on your coat, and cover it with his hair. He was smart.

Nancy's son, Max, really adored him. Max liked to call him "the Blob." He was a rather large cat in his prime of life. Molly and Nic were similar in size.

Harley for President

My other sister, Leslie, had several cats throughout her life. The latest was Harley. He was always dressed up in his "Harley Biker" clothes and ready for a picture. Harley was very kind when Molly came to visit. He would share his house with her and let her visit with the family.

Nancy and Max with Nic "the blob"

The Chattanooga Home Inspection Incident

I remember one day sitting in the kitchen waiting for the septic tank man to come and clean out the tank for an inspection. It was one of those inspections required by law to be done before your home goes on the market.

I heard the backhoe digging up the side yard and wondered why Annie was so quiet. I thought she was asleep on the upper deck. No, she was splashing around in the sewage in the back yard. I had never before seen a dog totally covered in fecal matter and the look of total surprise on the face of the man who was digging up the septic system.

To make matters worse, the house was to be shown in an hour to a couple moving to the area. Well, I had to find a place for one stinking dog to be held until the real estate man finished viewing the property with his potential buyers.

The garage would not work, because the smell would knock them unconscious, and the backseat of my car would not do this time around. So, off to the woods we went on a very long walk!

I cannot remember if that was the couple who bought the house. But the home was not on the market very long, and our relocation to Texas came up fast. Our homes always seemed to sell fast due to the unique settings on the water and in the woods. Being in the decorating business did help, too.

Annie getting a bath

Amber the Atlanta, Georgian
Golden Retriever

Amber, Our Southern-Belle

Amber was from Atlanta, Georgia. She was the first Golden Retriever we owned and adored. She was another smart dog. We had Amber living with us in our country home way out in Birchwood, Tennessee. We were living on the water again.

Amber enjoyed the lake as much as Annie. Amber was famous for her fishing skills. She was so patient and stood for hours staring into the water. One by one, she pulled the brim fish out of the local fishing hole. The fishermen were frustrated with her, because she caught more fish than all the fishermen on the docks.

My mother-in-law, Evelyn, was living with us one summer due to a knee injury. She called me to the front window over-looking the lake one day and yelled, "That dog is fishing."

I could not believe it. All around Amber's ankles, little fish flopped on the dock. Wow, she caught dinner for us! She became famous in the Tennessee River area, and her success continued on the next move to Lake Windward in Alpharetta, Georgia.

Evelyn had a Boston Terrier pug dog named Bonnie Babe. She also lived with us while Evelyn recovered. That dog did not like the water, but by the end of six weeks she overcame her fears and learned how to swim.

Our home was the playground for pups and big kids. Amber enjoyed the freedom of the big backyard and the Tennessee River before our move to Georgia. Her best friend was Jamie Lee, a Yellow Labrador Retriever that lived two doors away. Jamie Lee was so smart. She and Amber enjoyed swimming and fetching sticks together for hours.

Jamie Lee could also open the doors to our home. The day before the big move to Alpharetta we found Jamie Lee on our screened in porch. She must have been there over night, because the sadness in her eyes was beyond words. Jamie Lee was losing a great friend. Amber was her fishing buddy. This was a small lake neighborhood with only six houses on the street. A new dog friend would be hard to find.

We also had great neighbors, Betty and Whitey Larsen, who lived in a beautiful Spanish Style home out on the peninsula. They owned a little Terrier pup named Strudels. Strudels did not like the water. We learned the hard way about his swimming skills.

Mark and Whitey

Mark was playing with Strudels on our deck one beautiful Sunday afternoon. I remember it being a Sunday, because Mark was dressed in his new khaki slacks and dress shirt. As they played, I noticed Strudels in Mark's arms, and with one big toss, there went the dog into the water. All we saw were eyeballs-sinking eyeballs! Mark had to jump in and save him. Strudels really did not know how to swim. So much for the new Sunday clothes. But Mark had a new best friend.

We had Amber for only four years. When we moved to Alpharetta, Georgia with her the move changed her life forever.

Laynere, Stacie and Betty

Amber was not as happy in our new home in Alpharetta. She no longer had the lake in the back yard; we had to walk to the local fishing pier a couple blocks away. It was a nice walk for us, and yes, the lake did have fish. The little brim fish swam everywhere.

The local fisherman learned quickly that Amber was the best fishing dog in the area. Amber caught fish like a pro. She did not even hurt the fish as she stuck her head into the water and grabbed one right after another. The brim fish were in perfect condition for cooking. Amber was patient. She would even let the brim nibble on her fur, legs, and feet while she waited for the perfect time to pluck them from the water.

Her life was cut short by a misdiagnosis on a knee injury. Our local veterinary clinic had given her the medication 'bute,' which is short for butazone.

We took her to an orthopedic specialist in Marietta, Georgia and found out she was allergic to the medication. She died several days later at the University of Athens, Georgia.

It was one of the saddest days of our lives. We felt so helpless and misinformed. I have learned so much more through the years about researching canine medication and being more informed of the side effects. Our dogs were our children. Mark and I were unable to have children, so the four-legged ones were very close to out hearts.

Having Amber such a short time was so sad. She taught us how precious each day was with a Golden Retriever. Amber was one of the cleanest and

Baby Amber

most elegant dogs; she seldom got dirty and would drink and eat in a slow, calm way. I knew we would have another dog like her one day... well, maybe not.

Jamie Lee and Amber

Amber looking for brim

Amber fishing off the dock

Goodbye Amber

Texas Time-Ya'll Bring the Dawgs!

After several years of living on the lakes in Georgia and Chatta-nooga, it was time to move with a new job opportunity for Mark. This was a tough time for the dogs, the cat Pepper, and us. They loved the water and all of the activities that go hand in hand with water sports. I had never lived out west but was willing to try a new experience for Mark.

The weather was incredibly hot in the summer, but the winter months where glorious. The dogs had a pool in the backyard; that was fun for all of us… not as much fun as the lakes…but fun. Annie did well with the move. She enjoyed swimming every day and now had a white chlorine line all around her golden frame. She was always floating on a raft and soaking up the sun. Molly was not as happy with the pool. She enjoyed sitting on the pool steps and just getting half of herself wet.

They both had to learn about fenced in yards. I felt safer with them fenced in the backyard. The fences were black iron, and one could see out to the street very well.

The UPS and FED EX guys somehow knew Molly had arrived. She still knew that sound and knew their schedules.

I had to watch her more than ever, because the houses and roads where closer together… no more long winding driveway and trees hiding us from the world. This was Texas. It was hot, flat, treeless, and loaded with snakes, scorpions, and armadillos, especially on our walking trails.

Pepper spent most of her time in the house. She was uncomfortable with the surroundings and would only take walks with us in the evening. That was the cooler time of the day.

Unfortunately, we did not realize how dangerous these walks around the neighboring streets were becoming for our little group. The police had warnings posted about the coyotes running the streets at night, and to be careful with small animals and children.

It was around 9:00 p.m. and a beautiful clear night. I decided to take Annie, Molly, and Pepper for a stroll around the block. Mark was at a conference that evening in Dallas.

The first half of the walk was quiet, but the second half was a different story. The moon disappeared from the sky, and a slight wind started to pick up behind our backs. Immediately the cat was crying for me to come pick her up. She was probably nine years old now and not comfortable with us being away from the house. I stepped up my pace and headed back to pick her up; within seconds she just disappeared. Not a sign of her anywhere.

I ran up the street calling her name and continued to run down an abandoned trail between two houses to see if she was hiding. In the moonlight, there on an old barbed-wire fence, was a piece of her grey and black hair just sticking to the sharp clips that lined the barbed wire farm fence. Oh, this is not a good night, I thought.

I called my neighbors, Phil and Beverly, across the street, and the three of us went out to look for Pepper. There were signs of a struggle and cat hair on the fence, but no Pepper in sight.

At that moment I hated Texas and all its scary animals that hunted innocent pets in the nighttime. Phil suggested we look in the morning daylight and follow the old farm road to the dead end.

I knew this was going to be a rough couple of days. No sign of her the next morning at the breakfast feeding. No sign of her around the property. I walked up to the old trail and found pieces of her hair stuck to a barb wired fence that protected a wooded lane to the farm.

Poor, Pepper. The coyotes ran around the neighborhood that night, and I never should have walked around the block by myself. Pepper missed the safety of home in Tennessee, and now her life was over in a strange new place. I felt terrible. She was a sweet soul, and I felt the guilt of not protecting her better.

Pepper

The Land of Fences

Well, back to Miss Molly. One early morning after our great walk to the lake of Lewisville with both dogs, I thought I could finally catch up and get some interior design work done for a new home in our neighborhood.

The dogs were in the back yard cooling off by the pool, or so I thought. Molly had managed to wiggle her way out of the wrought iron fence and head towards the front of the house. Well, that is the street where the UPS trucks roam freely, and the diesel sounds fill the air.

I looked up, and to my horror, and I say horror, there in the street in front of my house was my little dog lying on her back, all four legs straight up in the air.

"Oh my gosh, what in the world has happened?" I said.

I grabbed the car keys and my bathrobe and ran up to the street to check on her. At that moment I heard a truck drive away, one street over.

"Oh no, she has been hit," I said.

I checked her breathing, and she just seemed to be knocked unconscious. Our veterinarian was in the office right down the street and said to please come right away. Her name was Dr. Denise Doolittle, (just like the Dr. Doolittle movies.) She was a Godsend. She grabbed Molly out of my arms and ran her in the back for tests.

It was only at that time I realized I was dressed in nightclothes, but it did not matter that day. I stayed with Molly until she woke up and started wagging her little white tail. The next thing she did was she sat up on her hind legs on the examination table and gave me a little doggie salute.

"What a trooper!" Dr. Denise said. "I think she is going to fine, so go home and change your clothes, and we will call you after lunch to pick her up."

Hurray! My little angel was going to survive this day after all. And yes, Annie was

Molly and the famous "sit up"

waiting for me at home with all of the tail wags and licks one could muster up!

Marilyn's Love of Dogs

Marilyn and Don Doudt were great neighbors who walked with us nightly. Their dog was named Doc. He was a Black Lab and a hint of Great Dane. He was aging fast. I could see the walks slowly starting to end. On a bad day, Marilyn would make a harness for Doc's back legs. The harness was a bath towel rolled into a long sling. It would take two of us to lift Doc. We would slide the towel under his stomach and on the count of three lift him into a standing position. This was the best way to get him outside to enjoy the warm sunshine.

Doc enjoyed scrambled eggs anytime of the day. He and I became buddies on the days Marilyn went to work. I headed over to their home, heated a frying pan, and scrambled eggs for him. He was such a gentle mannered dog.

Marilyn helped me several times with Annie and Molly when I had to go to work for our local Goodman Builders. There are memories of all of us walking to the lake and meeting up with two new pets, Frito and Heidi. They were Golden Retrievers and lived on the street behind us. All of us "dog people" stuck together and helped each other with house and dog sitting chores.

Marilyn started a rescue program for Airedales in the Dallas area. She was successful with her home placements. Marilyn was a soft-spoken girl who passed away at a young age. This book was a distant idea she and I talked about when we lived in Texas. She had just rescued Maggie another lost Airedale. We all loved her so... and her love of dogs was overwhelming. She will always be in my heart. Don, her husband, must miss her dearly.

Marilyn and Penny

Molly, the Texan

Molly did well with the bigger dogs, and they respected her. She was the tiny one with the big spirit. There was a new Golden Retriever, Shelly, that moved in one block behind us, and Molly really enjoyed Shelly's temporary small size of 20 pounds.

They played well and swam together in the evenings. All of the dogs shared the backyard swimming pools just like a bunch of little kids. The rafts in the pools were filled with lounging kids and puppies on the hot days. Some of the dogs even wore hats or visors.

We could walk all six of them at one time and never have to worry about them running off into the woods. They protected each other and stayed together while swimming in the lake, too.

Dallas was only going to be an eighteen-month stay for us. A new opportunity had surfaced for Mark in Houston, Texas. It was a good time to run a small machine shop and learn about the Texas market, so we decided to give it a try.

The hardest part of any move was saying goodbye again to great neighbors who had dogs and starting all over again in a new city. It was time to house hunt again.

"We must have a pool again for the dogs," I told Mark.

It was just too hot for them in the summer, and I wanted them to be able to swim again. Annie really enjoyed the water, and it would be easier for them to adapt to a new surrounding.

We found an older home in the Houston area called Lakewood Forest. It had a pool with fountains in the backyard (the fountains were decorative lions,) and a lake was across the street.

"Well, this is the best of both worlds," I told Mark.

The only tough thing about this neighborhood was the traffic one block away. The road was heavily traveled with commuter traffic early in the morning and late afternoon.

I found a church that backed up to a wooded area about three blocks away. It was perfect for walking and letting the dogs run free on the trails that were winding in and out of the woods. I hardly ever saw another soul in the area. It was great keeping Molly away from the busy roads that seemed to be an obsession with her little mind. The walks did us all good, and within a few months we settled in again.

It was not long before we met other dog walkers in the area, and soon it was time for picnics by the pool with new friends and their pets. During one of these parties the fence to the backyard was left open by mistake. I will never forget that moment when we realized Molly had gotten loose and was running up and down Jones Road (the busy commuter road) in the heavy traffic.

Mark was in a dead run, again. The cars on the road came to a full stop, and the nice people of Lakewood Forest stopped to help us. Molly was so excited to be out and about she never realized the danger she was causing.

Annie decided to follow her; she escaped through the back door in all of the excitement and ran with her on the busy road. Now we had both of them on the main road causing a traffic nightmare.

One of the couples we met at the park behind the church was spending the evening with us, and they had brought their two golden retrievers with them. Well, Molly made "the Big Escape" on Jones Road that evening, I believe, as a reaction to the other two dogs visiting at our home. I think Molly and Annie were upset having competition in the house.

The nice people of Houston stopped their cars and pulled off the highway. The dog run ended peacefully, thank goodness, because of the nice, polite people of Houston, Texas.

One-Eyed Jack

We had a lake full of Canadian geese across the street. One of the geese had lost an eye. We are not sure what happened to him. The neighborhood story had it that his name was Jack. One-Eyed Jack.

An angry man, who did not like the wildlife on the streets slowing the traffic, must have shot him. Jack did not like men. He liked women. He liked me. I noticed he was friendlier if I wore a skirt or shorts. If long pants were involved he would attack without warning.

Mark sat under the trees and fed the geese on Saturday mornings. Jack seemed to like Mark until one afternoon, when he decided to lower his long neck and chase Mark down the driveway. Mark turned sharply, slamming his knee into his car door. It was painful to watch, but on the other hand extremely entertaining to watch him run down the driveway with Jack on his tail. The car could be fixed. Mark's pride could not…

My friend Carol Thibodeau was visiting that summer with her two children, Jenny and Mike. Mike was standing in the driveway on a hot July afternoon. It was time for a swim. Jack decided to join us in the driveway, and out of the blue he just ran at Mike and stuck his beak into his swim trunks. He rammed his beak and face into Mike's swimsuit pocket and held on for dear life.

Carol and I were stunned. We had never seen anything like this… poor Mike. We screamed for Jack to let go, and Carol grabbed Jack's neck and pulled him away from Mike. Mike had a welt on his hip for the rest of the summer!

During the summer, Jack waddled across the street and walked to the mailbox with me. We walked side by side down the driveway. Mark always thought Jack looked like a little kid standing

He was tall and stood high next to my waist. He walked into the garage with me, and if I opened the kitchen door, he tried to walk right into the house. I knew the dogs would not be happy with this visitor.

Carol, Jenny, Mike Thibodeau and
Stacie and Mark with Annie & Molly

A Rough Move to Richmond, VA

Our Houston move came to an end after eighteen months. Mark and I went through some personal problems in our marriage around this time. We had moved so many times that I had a tough time with all of the relocating. Infertility problems, a serious back injury, and missing my family only made our relationship suffer more.

We decided to move closer to my home, which was Lancaster, Pennsylvania. The closest company that was hiring was in Virginia. I had heard wonderful things about Virginia, so Richmond would be the next stop in our lives.

Our house in Houston was on the market for a short time. The first day it was listed, it sold. We had not known how quickly our adventures in Texas would be over. We loaded up our jeep and started the cross-country trip with our two dogs.

I did not know our jeep's gas gauge was on recall and was not working correctly when we lived in Texas. We were on the Arkansas border with the air conditioner running full blast. The gas gauge registered about one quarter full but was really empty. We crossed over a very large span of a bridge, and the jeep just stopped running.

It was 100 degrees outside, and we had to wait for a tow truck to come rescue all of us. The dogs seemed fine. Mark and I were more stressed than usual, especially when we found out there was a recall on the gas gauge for that model. Thank goodness for warranties and AAA insurance. This trip took 22 hours.

Annie and Molly shared a bed with us in a local hotel that night, and two more nights on the trip. They were seasoned travelers. I know we were blessed with two well-behaved dogs.

My favorite Uncle Neal and Annie

Our move to Richmond was not a good one. Mark and I had a tough time with this one. It finally took a toll on our relationship.

I thought this would be a good time to settle into an apartment in my hometown of Lancaster, Pennsylvania and sort through all of the changes. The dogs stayed with me for a couple of months while Mark went on to Virginia to start his new job.

During this time I had back surgery for a ruptured disc. My parents and my Uncle Neal lived close by and could help with the dog walking and chores.

The separation time from Mark was not easy, and I could tell little Miss Molly missed her dad. Annie did fine but missed the big backyard, lakes, and pools. Living in an apartment complex was not for her. After several months of talking and rethinking our ideas with lawyers, Mark and I decided to work harder on our relationship.

Birkdale Golfing Community

We started the house-hunting project, again. This home had to be near woods and a lake, and it had to have good walking trails.

I drove through a neighborhood called Birkdale, and low and behold there were a lake, walking trails, a golf course, and large wooded lots. There was a community pool (but not for dogs!)

On one of the smaller side streets was a house for sale. It was tucked away in a cul-de-sac and had a wooded backyard. The yard was partly on the lake and partly on the fourth hole of the golf course. This was perfect for us.

Annie loved the backyard...she also loved chasing those stray golf balls! She found a very lovable beaver in the lake, too. We decided to call him Bucky.

Bucky answered when called...he slapped the water with his big wide tail and said hello to Annie and me. Annie and Bucky swam for about an hour in the evenings. I worried that Annie would get into trouble swimming so long, but she came home soaking wet and happy.

Mark could not believe how those two got along so well. Molly was not into swimming in the lake and getting all wet and smelly. She stayed on the bank with me and watched.

If Annie was out too long, Molly would start barking and running up and down the bank of the lake to let her know it was time to come home. I tried to videotape Annie and Bucky Beaver swimming, but it was too dark outside.

There was another house for sale on the street, and it was also on the lake. Well, two more canine friends soon joined in the fun. Digger and Hanna were Jack Russell Terriers, and they loved to play with my two dogs.

Molly's doggie friends could visit her easily and not have to worry about a busy street of car traffic. Hanna and Digger were her little play pals. The three of them took nice walks around the neighborhood in all kinds of weather. They were the Three Musketeers!

Hanna was named "Hannama Jack," from the sun tan lotion. Digger was named "Digger Odell," the name of the grave-digger from the old radio days. They were the cutest Jack Russell Terriers. The two of them could bark along to a Happy Birthday tune better than most of us could sing. They were the best dogs in the world and very entertaining.

The Jack Russell Terriers belonged to Nancy and Greg Odell, our best friends in Virginia. Nancy was a gorgeous red head and incredible cook. We always found her in the kitchen surrounded by her two little dogs at her feet looking for fallen scraps.

Molly and Annie loved to go over to their house, especially when it was cookout night. The steaks on the grill would sizzle in the moonlight. We would spend the evening on their back deck and sit at the picnic table under the stars. The view of the lake in the moonlight was breathtaking. The sounds of the crickets and birds made us feel like life could not get any better.

Life was good, and good friends made it even better…especially friends who enjoyed spending Friday or Saturday nights with all of the dogs. The pups loved to dance on the deck with us and listen to James Taylor, Country Western Songs, or whatever Greg Odell was in the mood for that evening.

Halloween night was always a fun time to dress up the dogs in Halloween Costumes. Mark and I enjoyed having a block party for the street. We set up tables and grills cooked hamburgers and hot dogs and handed out candy from the driveway. The neighbors brought the baked beans, potato salad, and various side dishes for the evening. The Irish Coffees were one of the favorites. The costumes for Hanna and Digger were two black and white skunk outfits. Molly was usually a ballerina, a pumpkin, or a Texas Cowgirl. We changed her costume several times in the evening. Christmas outfits for the dogs were allowed as we progressed into the holidays.

Hanna, Digger and Brazen

Digger

Nancy and Hanna

Digger

Mark started to travel back and forth to his new job in York. The trip was about five hours. Molly and I were once again together all through the week.

Molly

Nancy and Greg also had a hot tub on their back deck. The water was too hot for Annie; she became too high strung and ran around the deck and yard. But Molly enjoyed a dip while lying in my arms.

One afternoon Molly held up her paw and cried when we were getting out of the hot tub. Mark and I had noticed a couple of times when Molly jumped off the bed, her right shoulder hurt. This was the start of a problem that lasted for years.

There was a specialist in Richmond near the Cary Street area that ran some tests on Molly. She found Molly's right shoulder had not developed correctly when she was a puppy.

They did an ultrasound echo-cardiogram, ultrasound, cardiology consultation, radiographs, and blood pressure checks every 15 minutes. The little girl did so well considering the pain she was enduring. The diagnosis was shoulder instability. The shoulder blade dislocated out of the socket.

We had to discuss options to keep her comfortable.

The surgery would be a six-month recovery time. She would have a pin inserted into the shoulder for several months until the healing of the bones grew properly. The pin would come out after several weeks. She would have to live in the laundry room for months with limited activity, which meant no walks to the lake.

The medication for the pain was Rimadyl, and it worked for awhile. We had a lot of decisions to make. Molly was about ten years old at this time.

Annie was approximately 8 years old, and her golden face started to become white, especially around her eyes and nose. She was slowing down. But swimming with the beaver kept her in good shape, and she stayed well.

One afternoon in October I heard a scrapping noise at the front door. It was a strange noise, and I had to look down the foyer to the windows that bordered the door. All I could see were black deer hooves sticking straight up in the air! What in the world?

Annie had found a deer carcass in the woods behind our house. The body was still intact, and the legs were as straight as an arrow pointing to the heavens. Annie was so proud of her find.

"Oh, I hope I can find some garbage bags big enough to fit this body into it!" I said. This would look very odd sticking out of the garbage can, I thought. I knew the odor would collect in the garage, too. I thought we would take a little ride to the landfill and get rid of this deer before Mark got home.

Annie was disappointed when I drove off with her prize deer wrapped in black plastic bags. I felt like a gangster in an old movie... getting rid of the evidence from a crime scene.

I was never surprised by the road kill Annie found to make a quick meal for herself. She was fed well at home but always came up with something in the woods that obviously tasted better.

Annie

The Outer Banks

Mark and I took both dogs to the Outer Banks the following spring. That was their first experience with salt water, and all that the beach had to offer surprised them: the waves in the ocean, the cool breeze, and how yucky the water tasted.

The evenings were spent walking on the beach trying to catch the Ghost Crabs that only surfaced at night and bit us on our toes. Wow, that hurt! The crabs hung on Annie's noise as she developed a quick skill of tossing them over her neck- that made them go flying! This technique worked well, and Annie taught it to Molly. The two of them were able to catch crabs for us. A few where flattened and swallowed by the turning tides. The seagulls followed us and enjoyed a few nibbles from the leftover crabs. The good leftovers went into a bucket to be steamed.

The beach allowed the dogs to swim in the surf with us during the day. Annie loved the ocean. It was hard for us to swim with her, because she would swim and "claw up" our backs. Mark's back and arms were covered with scratches. She swam out into the surf and followed us everywhere we swam. She enjoyed the water and rode the waves like a true surfer.

We took the dogs home to cool off from the afternoon sun and to drink regular water. It was too hot for the dogs to be out in the afternoon heat. They relaxed in the air conditioning and waited until the sun set to go back and hunt for the Ghost Crabs.

Our vacation was fun with them. It was like taking care of two little kids at the beach.

During our vacation at the Outer Banks we noticed Molly was not walking as fast as usual.

"I think her shoulder is out of place, again. I think keeping her quiet and out of the water will help for awhile," I said.

Mark was able to realign it again and keep her quiet in the cool comfort of the air conditioning. Pain medications helped keep her comfortable for the rest of the week. We both watched over her and walked quietly next to her on all outings.

I noticed Molly's little shoulder bothering her more often. The specialist showed us how to manipulate the shoulder back into place without having her cry out in anguish. We started carrying pain medicine for her at all times. If we could realign the shoulder in a short amount of time, the less the pain would be for her. If we could realign it before getting to the veterinary clinic or emergency room, the less pain for her. This became a way of life for us. We found steps for her to climb up onto the bed.

Molly let us know if she felt her shoulder slip out of the socket.

The specialist recommended a surgery that would keep her immobile in a crate for 6 weeks. She would be able to go outside to do her business, but that was it…no walking or running. There would be a pin in her shoulder, and it would stay there until the shoulder was healed. After that a second surgery would be required to remove the pin.

Oh, Molly. She was so precious. We decided against the surgeries and prayed we could keep her quiet and safe for the next couple of months. We needed some time to think about her treatment plan.

Miss Molly and Stacie at the beach

Annie in the surf

Molly's Shoulder Pain

Nancy Odell and I still enjoyed the hot tub with the furry kids after our return trip home. We even allowed Molly to sit on my knees and lay in the water. After letting her out of the tub, she held her little paw up in the air. I thought the weight of the water had pulled her shoulder out again. But, no … she just wanted to go home and be with Mark.

She knew he was cutting the grass, and if she limped toward him, she knew he would stop the yard work and spend time with her. Molly also knew how to make me look like a bad mom.

We had a few more scares with her shoulder that fall. We made a veterinary appointment with Dr. Bill's Veterinary Hospital.

"It appears the shoulder never grew properly together. The shoulder slips out of place." Dr. Bill explained to us.

The shoulder might have needed a pin inserted into the bone to hold it together. It was to be a painful procedure, and Molly would be isolated in our laundry room for weeks.

I met with the specialist again in Richmond for a second opinion. The specialist in downtown Richmond had two options. We could do the shoulder surgery or not do it.

I made an appointment the following week for several tests for Molly. I would have to drop her off early in the morning and come back early afternoon to pick her up.

She was sedated but happy, and her little tail wagged when I got into the exam room. She is a little trooper! The doctors and I, along with Mark, decided not to schedule her surgery for her shoulder. We decided to watch over her the next couple of months and see how she did with the Rimadyl for pain. We also kept Tramadol Hydrorchloride on hand for severe pain. Our daily walks were not as brisk, but Molly was able to walk with Annie all around the block.

Molly and Casey

Bucky Beaver Is Back

My little kids both started to show some age. The yellow fur around Annie's eyes was all of a sudden a whitish color. Her nose started to turn white, too. Annie was about nine now, and Molly about six.

Annie seemed to enjoy resting more in the bushes by the front door. She could see everything going on down the street and visit with all the dogs walking by. Of course, a nice dip in the lake in the backyard was a plus on a hot day.

Annie surprised us one evening with a burst of energy. It was dusk, and the lake was quiet and dark. All of a sudden a loud slapping sound hit the water. It was the beaver. There went our Golden Retriever, Annie, for a swim with the beaver.

The beaver's tail hit the water with a loud thud, and Annie swam off, around and around in a circle with the beaver. The two of them were out in the middle of the lake for over an hour. The moonlight reflected their silhouettes in the water. I do not think anyone ever believed that my dog swam with a beaver that we continued to call Bucky.

Bucky built a nest for his family in the winter months, and Annie was his friend. This ritual went on for several months, at least until the lake was almost frozen in the middle of the winter. We called Bucky's name in the evenings to see if he wanted to go for a swim with Annie. He answered with a loud thud of the tail on the water. This was good exercise for Annie… and I did not have to walk her around the block every night.

Annie and Molly were buddies. They even tolerated Casey, our new cat.

Casey sat in the window of a pet store next to the hair salon where I got my hair cut. A family who was moving out of state abandoned him, because they could not take him along. He was a cute, yellow-orange tabby cat.

I wondered if purchasing a cat was a good idea. We had the best cat, Pepper, for years, and she did well with the dogs. Well, it was time to get Mark's opinion again on the adoption idea.

Mark went with me the following day to look at Casey. Casey had the original name of Socks. All of his toes were white, and around his neck was a v-neck marking of white fur; he was very handsome. This yellow-orange cat reminded me of the litter of kittens we cared for in Houston, Texas.

Annie, our Golden Retriever, had found them under a trailer in the parking lot by our church. They were starving and cold and needed to be inside with the winter weather on its way. I remember getting a box and putting them inside my car for the short ride home.

Mark and I took them to our local veterinary clinic the next day. One of the kittens was not doing well and had to be put to sleep.

There were only three left, and they were adopted quickly. A little girl down the street adopted the tiny tabby cat that looked like our

Casey; she had asked her mother if she could name it "Stacie," after me. I was honored!

Friends of Mark adopted the other orange tabby kitten. They had a horse farm out in the country with a big old barn that a cat would love. It was a perfect place for a cat. That cat was also named Casey. He loved horses and spent hours sitting on the fences rubbing against the horses as they lined up along the fences to be fed.

Well, I guessed our Casey was going to be the newest member of our family. Mark picked him up and put him in our van with Annie and Molly. The ride home was full of sniffs and nudges from our two dogs, checking out the strange new family addition in the crate.

I remember Mark opened the crate in the living room with the two dogs on either side of him.

"Well, here goes," Mark said, as he opened the crate's door to introduce the cat.

Casey

Casey rolled over on his back and let the two dogs sniff him all over. That was all it took. Casey was smart. He knew these two would not attack him. They had the perfect opportunity to gobble him up, but they licked him and welcomed him into our home.

Our life in Richmond was going well. The neighbors were nice, and they enjoyed the dogs, too. We had an occasional run-in with the local golfers. Annie and Molly loved to run and greet the golfers on the fourth hole, which was in our back yard. The only thing dividing our yard from the course was a couple of trees. After a quick dip in the lake, Annie would run and greet them and shake the loose water off her fur onto the well-dressed golfers. I cannot remember how many lectures I got from the "golf police," but most of the golfers laughed off the antics of a happy-go-lucky dog.

Molly's shoulder started to worry me more and more. We had several scares over the next couple of months with the shoulder slipping out of place. I knew the surgery would be tough on her, because she was about ten years old now. We took more and more precautions with her walks. We spent more time with Dr. Bill's Pet Infirmary for medical advice and check ups. We were regular patients visiting the office every couple of weeks.

Hurricane Isabel

The hurricane in the fall of 2003 destroyed Richmond, Virginia. Mark and I sat at the airport packed and ready to go to Newport, Rhode Island for a weekend of sailing. I felt I could not get on the airplane. The man on the radio kept saying this was going to be one of the worst storms ever to hit this area. We had a dog sitter at the house. Theresa Phillips was on call and was the favorite pet sitter in our neighborhood. But the weather report for the high winds and trees falling on power lines could make it impossible for her to get to our home.

I jumped in the car and headed back to the house to be with Annie, Molly, and Casey. Mark went on to Newport, Rhode Island.

The power went out at 3:00 p.m. in the afternoon, and it was dark outside. I remember the howling wind and the rain falling so heavily it looked like it was raining sideways. A tree fell on our roof in the middle of the night. It was a huge oak tree outside our bedroom window. Fortunately another tree broke its fall, and it landed gently on our bedroom roof above my closest. That could have been a mess.

The dogs and I slept very little that night. I was able to go next door and get Nancy and Steve Bordeaux to help me climb into the attic and check for damages. Steve hammered blue tarps on the weakened areas to keep most of the water out of the attic.

We kept going next door to check on our neighbor, Herb. We had our flashlight and candles, so we could walk down his long winding driveway and not trip and fall on all the downed branches and trees. Herb was out in the driveway in the middle of the night with a chain saw trying to clear the driveway to make a small walking path to the house.

Molly waiting for Mark

I will never forget the high winds and the driving rain that night. We had to change into dry clothes every half hour. The trees fell like dominos in the back yards. The sound of the falling trees shook the ground and windows with such force it felt like a war zone.

We ended up cooking on a gas stove for days. The power was out for a week. Annie and Molly and I checked on Herb every couple of hours, and meals were sent over until we could get out of the neighborhood to grocery shop or go to Bob Evan's or the Cracker Barrel.

Mark returned home the next afternoon. He had rented a car near Philadelphia with several men who lived in the Virginia area. The Philadelphia Airport was the closest airport for available rental cars for our area. He kept calling along the way to see what supplies were needed…mostly ice and water.

Theresa Phillips was our pet sitter and on call most of the time we lived on Merseyside Lane. She dog and cat sat more times than I could ever count. She spent several nights at our home while I traveled on some of the business trips with Mark.

I had met Theresa through a mix-up with a local pet sitting company. We were away and had called a local pet sitting service in Richmond, and the sitter never arrived that evening. I was in a panic and called a friend, who recommended Theresa Phillips and her friend Suzanne. The two of them came to the house at 9:00 p.m. that night and walked both Annie and Molly in the darkness along the path side of the golf course. I am sure there was a bit of a mess to clean up in the house. She never complained. She was incredible and a huge help.

We decided it was easier for her to take both dogs to her home on several occasions. She had two dogs, Duncan and Willie, and they got along well with Annie and Molly. Willie was a Dandy Din Mont Terrier, but Duncan- we were not sure about. He was certainly a well-loved mutt. Both of the dogs came from the SOS Shelter in Richmond. We believe it stood for Save Our Shelters.

I am sure Molly ran the house when Duncan and Willie were home. Theresa said Molly would growl at Duncan and Willie when she had enough of their running around the coffee table. Molly did not like them sniffing her "private parts" and would stop them in their tracks with a growl if they got too close. She could handle herself with the big dogs!

I had to work on some design projects, and Theresa's help allowed me to get out of the house and get some work done. She was an angel. I think of her often and wish we could still spend time with her.

She continued her pet sitting business (mostly cats) after we moved and went on to work for a bank in downtown Richmond. A job with real people!

I know Molly loved to go for car rides out in the Virginia countryside with Theresa. They would go visit her mom at the family farm. I am sure they had special times together. Molly always came home from Aunt Theresa's special trips with a goody bag.

Willie and Duncan

Losing Annie

Annie was the most hysterical animal I had ever been around. She kept us laughing with her antics in the water, mud, and septic tanks, and chasing skunks, deer, and beavers. She lived life to the fullest and had fun along the way.

I noticed her slowing down and spending more time sleeping in the front yard in the bushes. She had developed a small, quarter size bump below her rib cage. Our vet thought it was a fatty tumor and told us not to worry about it unless it got really large. The large tumors end up growing into the muscle and surrounding tissues. They are not painful.

I knew she ate a lot of bad things in the woods when we were not around- mostly dead and decaying animal body parts. Living next to the woods was a challenge for us. Trying to keep a watchful eye on her all of the time was difficult. I really believe she developed some stomach problems before we knew it.

Mark called me to the garage one fall morning and said Annie had been ill most of the morning. She was in the garage and started to vomit. It was not the normal vomit; it was dark red. She was bleeding somewhere in her stomach.

We rushed her to the clinic that Saturday morning. Dr. Steve said it would be best to keep her there all afternoon for observation. He thought it might just be a stomach virus.

Mark and I left her there for the day. That evening we decided to go out to dinner with Nancy and Greg, our neighbors.

I never heard my cell phone ring that evening. I guess it was too noisy in the restaurant. Dr. Steve had called to tell us that he went back to check on her in the early afternoon, and she had passed away. He could not believe how quickly she went.

I could not stop crying. I never got to say goodbye to this wonderful pet, this pet that had lived life to the fullest and had loved living on the lake chasing beavers and skunks, and rolling in septic tank crud. She always made us smile and laugh.

I remember spending the rest of the evening sitting on the deck with our neighbors, in total shock, just staring at the stars. Annie had been eleven years old, going on twelve, and was the sweetest Golden Retriever next in line to Amber. My Golden Retrievers did not live very long, but they sure taught us a lot about life. Never take life too seriously. I think I spent the whole month in shock, depression and sadness.

Mark and I spent the next couple of months in a deep sadness. The holidays would never be the same. Our Christmas cards always had the dogs dressed up in a holiday outfit with Santa. Santa was always at the pet stores or the local mall. We had a picture made every year. Some of our neighbors were good photographers, too.

It took several days for Molly to realize she was now the number one dog in the house. She kept looking around and under furniture and finally realized the house was all hers except for Casey, the cat.

She was now the alpha dog and could sleep in our bed right smack in the middle on her special soft blankets. Her little stuffed toys lined her blankets like a little cradle. Her front paws stretched out into Mark's back, and her hind paws were stretched out toward my arms.

Molly was now about nine and a half years old with the bad shoulder. We found a "horse step" that she could use to make it easy to climb into the bed with us. We actually had two steps for her, one to keep by the car and one to keep by the bed.

She loved to travel with us and always enjoyed room service and a little visit with the maids. The chefs in the hotels sometimes made her a nice breakfast of eggs and sausage. All the staff adored her. It was her cute little face that made her hard to resist. She loved to sit at the front desk and greet the new guests as they checked into their rooms.

Her favorite Marriott hotel was in downtown Chattanooga, Tennessee, where she could visit her old house, walking trails, and neighbors. I really believe she remembered the area, even with all of the relocations.

After returning home to Richmond, Molly enjoyed the quiet little walks up the street. We first stopped and walked up the steps to the back deck of Nancy and Greg's home in the moonlight. There Digger and Hanna greeted us, and Molly got a treat from Nancy's kitchen before bedtime.

Next, we walked further up the street to Liz Elkovitch's front door. A container of doggie bones sat by the front door for Molly. She picked the snack of the evening, and I would break the small bone in half. One part was buried in her front yard for a snack later, and the other part was eaten on the way back home. That was our new routine after the passing of Annie. Molly was well taken care of by the Merseyside neighbors.

I also remember Jean and Herb Bailey, who lived next door to us. Jean was taken ill while we lived there and spent several weeks in her bedroom.

One summer evening Molly visited with Herb on his front porch. I walked over to visit with them, and Herb told me Molly was in the house with Jean.

"I think Molly is under the bed," Herb laughed. "Jean is sound asleep and does not realize Molly is in there with her."

I remember crawling half way under the bed to wake up Molly and take her home. I did not want to awaken Jean or give her a scare in the darkened room.

Molly loved to follow Herb around the living room and keep him company. She was such a good friend. Herb's grandchildren loved to play with Molly too, particularly Logan.

Logan

Molly and Me

Moving Home to Lancaster, PA

Mark and I had some serious discussions about moving closer to my parents in Lancaster, Pennsylvania. There was a job opening in York, Pennsylvania that was only 45 minutes away from Lancaster County.

It was a difficult time for us, and another move for Molly and Casey would not be easy. Molly watched the packers and furniture movers lift every piece of our history and move it out of the house. She sat at the top of the stairs and stared in disbelief at the changes occurring in front of her little nose. Casey ran away into the woods behind the house and watched from a distance. He did show up on moving day and allowed us to put him in his travel kennel. They are smarter than we give them credit for.

During the long, five-hour ride to Lancaster, I noticed how quiet Molly became. We stopped for a light lunch and a small walk and let her stretch her legs at a picnic area.

Shortly after our rest stop, Molly crawled under the dashboard where the cool air conditioning was blowing on her back. After a few minutes I noticed her four little feet moving in unison, like she was swimming. She was in a trance, and I believed she was having a seizure.

I stopped the car and pulled into a gravel driveway somewhere in the Gettysburg area. I lifted Molly onto the cool grass. She was breathing but seemed a little confused. I held her for a few minutes, and when I finally got my wits together, found my cell phone lying on the gravel road. It must have fallen out of the car when I carried Molly to the ground.

Mark drove separately in the truck and had the cat in the crate. I called Mark and asked him to back track and come check on us. He told me the cat was ill, too.

I also called the veterinarian at Neffsville Veterinary Clinic in Pennsylvania, near our new hometown. Carol, the greeter at the clinic, and Dr. George Nylan were waiting for us on the other end.

I think this move was all too much for Molly's little heart to bear. I was so scared for her; it was all I could do to drive on to our new vet clinic. We made good time, and Molly was checked out immediately. She was given some blood tests and medications called Phenobarbital and Enalapril Maleate. We also added Lasix as the weeks progressed.

After settling into our home, Molly seemed to be calmer. She still had the occasional seizure, but they were very short, and the medications helped. Sometimes Molly came to stand by my feet if she did not feel well. I would sit with her before the seizure would start. She was an amazing little friend.

There were several more episodes of her little shoulder slipping out of the socket. One afternoon she fell down the front steps. I think her eyesight was starting to fail. She hobbled up the steps to my side, and I picked her up and drove off to the vet, again.

This time, Dr. Nyland suggested we put her shoulder in a sling. She wore the sling for six weeks. I had to walk with her and carry her up the stairs and outside to do her business. It was wintertime, and our walks were not very long anyway.

"I think we need a wagon to pull her around the neighborhood, so she can go visit her doggie friends," Mark suggested.

We borrowed one from our neighbors, and Molly really did not like it. She just wanted to be held and do little walks around our block.

We kept her on the Rimadyl, and when the pain worsened we switched her to Tramadol. We found stair-steps for her to climb up onto our bed and another set to keep by the bedroom window. Her life was all about comfort at this time, and my sanity.

I had completely lost track of all of the visits to the veterinary clinic. Becky Bitzer, the Client Relations Specialist, would meet us in the parking lot on several occasions and hold Molly in her arms to calm her down. Molly did not like going into the building and would get the shakes so badly we could hardly hold onto her. The last thing I needed was a seizure.

Molly's favorite time was our little walks around the Veranda neighborhood. She visited with the dogs on every street. So enjoyed Cody, Charlie, Archie, Zoe, Lily, Ginger, Paris and a few other buddies.

My mom and dad have a Yellow Labrador across the street from them named Mercedes. He belongs to Jill Walls, and Molly and Mercedes were good friends in that neighborhood.

Mercedes was very gentle with Molly. The two of them really enjoyed my mom's pot roast and the goodies she would cook up in the kitchen. Molly would sit on the side porch at my parent's home and watch all of the dogs walk by.

Molly also spent grooming time with Cyndi Cox, from Just 4 Petz. Cyndi came to the house for the haircuts. Cyndi worked in a large van that made a beeping sound when backing into the driveway. The sound must have reminded Molly of the UPS truck from the good old days.

But as age crept in, Molly was scared of the noise and would run and hide under the bed. It was a large king size bed, and I could not

reach her to pull her out safely from underneath the middle of the bed. So, that appointment was usually cancelled.

I had to hold her tightly in my arms until Cyndi was settled in and ready to cut her hair. She always added beautiful bows and bandannas. Molly was adorable and spent the afternoon walking around the neighborhood with me to show off her new haircut and bows.

Molly and her new haircut

During some of the business trips with Mark, we had to hire Joyce Congleton to stay with Molly and Casey overnight. Joyce had a company called Paws at Home, and she is a great dog and cat sitter. We had to go over the medication checklist with Joyce before we left town for a couple of days.

Molly loved Joyce and enjoyed her company, especially in the middle of the night when she was scared or did not feel well. Joyce brought over her favorite book, pillow and pajamas. She and Molly would watch movies late into the night.

I noticed Molly developed a dry cough in the evenings. It was called a cardiac cough. It was one more condition to watch and check on each day. We had such a wonderful support team with her. I could never thank all of friends and neighbors for their help.

Casey also developed a new personality. He was the lone survivor of the dogs in our home. He developed a high-pitched meow that meant 'open the door and let me out now.' He then traveled from front door to side door to garage door demanding to come back in the house. His visit lasted a few minutes, just enough time for a snack of Fancy Feast and a small nibble of dry food, and then Casey would come to us again to let him out.

This game went on throughout the day and sometimes during the night, if we heard him. He learned to push his little paw under the closed bedroom door and shake the door with all his might. He meowed loudly or screamed at us if we did not get up and let him outside. This antic usually took place around 3:00 a.m. Finally, we made a small bed in the garage with snacks to hold him over through the night. That gave us a break.

Delaware Beach

Mark and I made a reservation to go to Delaware beach in the early fall months. We found a beach house that was pet-friendly. This home was three levels and lots of stairs. We closed off all of the stairs and slept and lived on one floor. That worked out the best for us.

Molly enjoyed the decking and especially the sun porch. There was a cool ocean breeze and gorgeous view. Mark enjoyed his coffee and cigar in the morning air with sweet little Molly at his side. We carried her to the beach, and she was able to walk in the sand.

Our evening dinners were usually take-out, so we could spend time with Molly in the house. I was always afraid to leave her alone for any length of time because of a seizure. But our week was relaxing and was enjoyed by the three of us.

We enjoyed the home so much, that we rented it one year later with our Molly. We never thought this second trip would be the last one with her at the beach. She was fourteen years old now. I never thought we would be on a vacation without her company.

Molly's Quiet Times

Molly's time with us was slowly coming to an end. I knew she was not feeling 100% most of the time, but Cindy, our groomer, loved to come to the house and groom her and put little decorative bows in her ears. Molly was still the little beauty queen with the bows in her ears and a matching bandanna. We would change them every month, and whatever holiday was celebrated that month corresponded with the decorating of her ears!

Cindy was with Molly during her last couple of hours on this earth. Molly was bathed and adorned in yellow bows, and as the afternoon wore on, she became quiet and started to shiver. I sat with her at the top of the steps and started to wonder if she was in pain. I called the vet clinic and asked if I could bring her in again. Something was wrong, and I knew her shoulder was not out of place.

We spent some time in the Comfort Room at the clinic with Misty and Becky. It was comforting to reminisce about Molly and all of the good she had brought into our lives. The Comfort Room had an oriental rug on the floor, a comfortable sofa, and lamps and pictures on the wall. It was a quiet, wonderful room for prayer or meditation.

The vet tech looked Molly over in the exam room.

"Oh, my, look at this lump on the gum line in her mouth," she said.

It looked like a tumor was wrapped around a tooth. Oh, this is not good, I thought. Maybe some type of oral cancer has suddenly shown up in her mouth. She did not have the best teeth to begin with, and we only had her teeth cleaned once in her little life. She was probably a good candidate for teeth problems, but the anesthesia was a serious issue with her seizure and heart problems. I thought she was just starting to feel ill.

Dr. Nyland administered a pain patch on her back to give her pain relief.

"She should feel better by the time you get her home. Keep her quiet and watch her around stairs," he said.

Mark was driving in that night from Pittsburgh to see her and spend some time with her. The moment we got home, Molly ran straight up the stairs to see if Mark was home. I held her in my arms and told her to slow down, no running up and down the stairs. But her little spirit was willing to search the house for her dad.

We also had pain medications for her to take as soon as the patch started to wear off. I held her most of the evening, and she was able to eat a little dinner and drink water. That was a good sign. I prayed to God that night to please keep her alive until morning, so Mark could spend some time with her.

She slept by my side most of the night. In the early morning hours she ran down the hallway and started going potty in the house. Blood came out of her, and she seemed weak. I wrapped her in a blanket, and we sat outside in the garage and waited for Mark's return from Pittsburgh. She seemed happy and content to just sit with me.

I had loved this little girl for 15 years, and now our time together was coming to an end. What an amazing journey. This little Cockapoo was my whole life. She was my companion when Mark traveled and my little passenger on all of the trips across country. We were best buddies.

Mark arrived, and we spent the afternoon in the garage with Molly, taking turns holding her and comforting her. By the end of the day, we knew it was time to take her to the clinic. The doctor on call was waiting for us.

We went to the veterinary office and into the Comfort Room for our last good-byes. It was really peaceful and comforting for us, and Molly was not in pain, due to the pain patch. She really looked calm and comfortable. Her little tail wagged in the crook of the doctor's arm. I think she knew it was her time to go to Heaven. We collected her little bows and collar and sat with her until the doctor finished the procedure.

"Her heart has stopped," he whispered. She looked like a little sleeping puppy.

My life stopped that day, and all of the memories of all the stories came flooding back to me. She was the lost dog- the stray no one wanted. She kept our family together through all of the moves and marital problems. She was my hero! Rest well, my little friend.

Molly my little hero!

Afterword

Molly received fifteen flower arrangements the following week and cards and letters from every state we ever lived in and called home. I will share some of the notes with you. Molly passed away on May 1, 2009.

Molly's painting by Judy Beck Lobos

My dear friend, Judy Beck Lobos, painted a portrait of Molly. It was the most precious gift I have ever received, and I will treasure it forever. Judy can be contacted for pet portraits at: judybecklobos.com

There was one card that stands out and sums up Molly's personality. It is a perfect way to end this story:

Dear Mark and Stacie:

We will always remember Molly with fond and loving memories, as she was the first to greet us to Drake Lane three years ago. She never passed us by without stopping to say hello, a true southern lady who was loved by all. Thank you for letting us share in her life.

With love, Ken and Phyllis (Lancaster, PA)

We also heard from friends all over the country:

Dear Stacie and Mark:

We're so sorry for your loss… Molly was so blessed to have you both and I am sure she's up in "Doggie Heaven" bragging about her fabulous life in your loving care!! Saver the memories and let them help you heal, meantime, take care of each other always.

Fondly,

Terri, Dick & Cody, too! (Alpharetta, GA)

"I am in the birds that sing,

I am in each lovely thing ... "

And I will live in your heart forever.

Know that Molly was loved and is safe in doggie heaven now ...

Molly has earned her wings!!!!

Love,

Harley, Leslie and Dan (Centerville, VA)

> *From the poem "Do Not Stand at My Grave and Weep"*

Dear Friends:

I am so very sorry to hear Miss Molly passed away. I know so well the emptiness you are feeling, and all I can say is Molly was a lucky dog to have such a wonderful family, and you were equally lucky to have such a special furry friend to share your life. I share in your sadness and love you both. I keep you in my prayers and miss you. My deepest sympathy to you.

Love, Ameta (Dalton, GA)

Dear Reader:

After sitting down to write this book about Molly, Annie, Casey, Pepper, and Amber, my four-legged children, I felt some closure to all of the love and caring Mark and I went through with these wonderful pets. Molly went through so much with her illnesses. She was certainly a joy to be around even in those final days.

For many months, I wrote about her in the middle of the night. I wanted to tell her story to my family, my friends, and to anyone who would listen. She made us laugh, and cry. She was my furry friend through all of the moves, a companion at my feet and reason to get up in the morning. I will never forget her... she was a great dog.

My special thanks to Mark for letting me cover the kitchen table for months with photos and notes and stories of our "kids"... and to my parents, thank you for being such dog lovers and teaching me how to care for these wonderful pets. They had many laughs with us especially during boating season on the Tennessee River with two dogs.

The unconditional love and the wonderful friends we met through the years of dog and cat parenting will remain in my heart forever. Molly found us, and she kept us together as a family. I will never forget her strong will to live and to be my companion during all of the storms our family weathered through...

Molly passed away May 1, 2009

Our deepest thanks to Dr. George Nyland and the Staff at Neffsville Veterinary Clinic for the excellent care of our dear pets. Dr. George Nyland spent 38 years caring for animals at Neffsville Veterinary Clinic. In honor of Dr. George the clinic has instituted the George B. Nyland Injured Animal Fund. If you would like to participate in this fund, donations may be made by sending a check made payable to the "Neffsville Veterinary Clinic" with a notation on the memo line of "George B. Nyland Injured Animal Fund." Dr. George Nyland retired December 2010. He will be missed dearly by the Self Family.

Neffsville Veterinary Clinic
2555 Lititz Pike
Lancaster, PA 17601
717-569-5381
www.neffsvillevet.com

Coming soon.... LULU our new cockapoo!!!